# The Paradigm Shifter

# The Paradigm Shifter

*450 Motivational And Inspirational Quotes, That Will Revolutionize Your Life Both Literally & Spiritually*

Kenneth (Kenny) Chiverton

**Kenneth (Kenny) Chiverton**
**The Paradigm Shifter**

Published by Spines Publishing Platform
ISBN: 979-8-89383-466-6

# Preface

This book is written to encourage, inspire, and build you up to become the person that you should be by the way of Positive Thinking; the saying and quotes are derived from both Spiritual and Literal Inspirations.

As a Minister of God's Infallible Word for the past 40 years and an entrepreneur for the past 26 years, I am totally persuaded that everything which is written in this book will enhance the way of life of every reader that read it and make as much of the contents applicable to their personal lives.

It is a fact that none of us knows everything, but all of us know something.

So, with absolute humility, I must say that it is incumbent upon me to share with you, and to impart to you in this book some of the things that I have been Impacted with.

(Main Quote)

The Paradigm Shift that you need to propel you into your desired future will start in your mind. It is the positivity of your thinking that will enhance the positivity of your saying, and the positivity of your saying will empower the positivity of your doing.

So, my Brothers and Sisters, Family and Friends, it is incumbent upon all of us to Think Positively, for there is stupendous victory in Positive Thinking.

The mind is the governor of the body and the CEO of our actions. Where the mind goes, the body will follow.

(1)

If you want to hear well done at the end of your life's journey,
then make sure that you have done well while living it.

(2)

People who always try to stop you from going somewhere are
mainly those who aren't going anywhere, stay focused and
keep on keeping on.

(3)

Loyalty is always rare, so please endeavor to keep it whenever
it is extended to you.

(4)

Meekness is not a symbol of being weak; but it is actually
strength under control.

(5)

The bitter things in your life that cause you to live in hate are
the same things that you need to eliminate.

(6)

The prerequisite of sadness is bad news, but the prerequisite
of gladness is good news; be careful with what or who you
listen to.

(7)

People will talk about you if you are making a difference, they will try to hinder you if you are doing something good, and they will try to stop you if you are going somewhere; be prepared for the scrutiny.

(8)

There are some bad ways in the best of us, and there are some good ways in the worst of us, so all of us have to continuously work on ourselves individually.

(9)

Don't let your failures of the past determine your victories in your present or your triumphs of your future; continue to think positively.

(10)

Real freedom is not the right to do what we want to do, but it is the prerogative to do what we should.

(11)

Don't be afraid of failure, but rather be terrified of having regrets because you gave up when you should have held on.

(12)

Everyone won't become famous, but everyone can become effective in their environments and their communities.

(13)

In your Life's journey, you will hear more No than Yes, but don't let a negative mindset overwhelm you; the life-transforming YES is coming soon.

(14)

Yesterday is your history; learn from it. Tomorrow is your destiny; look to it. But today is your victory; rejoice in it.

(15)

Your setback of today is a setup for your comeback of tomorrow, so don't give up, don't give out, don't give in; your victory is imminent.

(16)

Your ability is predicated upon what you are capable of doing; your motivation is determined by what you do, but it is your attitude that will determine how high you go.

(17)

It is always better for us to seek to understand than for us to seek to be understood.

(18)

Making tangible sacrifices will always bring you timely solutions.

(19)

Living for God is not a monumental task, but it is an amazing privilege.

(20)

Having a vast amount of education and knowledge is a great blessing to you, but it will become a greater blessing when you impart it to others.

(21)

In your quest for exceptionalism, you will have criticisers and congratulators, but it is imperative that you accept them on both sides of the spectrum, for they will help propel you into your destiny.

(22)

Sometimes we will be more affected by the silence of our friends rather than the words spoken by our enemies.

(23)

You should never try to decrease your goals but always try to increase your effort in achieving them.

(24)

Learn to do what you can in the place where you are and with the limited resources that you have, and make the best of it.

(25)

We cannot place a monopoly on the God of our salvation, but we have the prerogative to place a monopoly on the salvation of our God; Salvation is free, claim it, embrace it and monopolize it.

(26)

Creativity and ingenuity are the two main objectives that will help a nation to rise from poverty to prosperity.

(27)

Learn to speak positive faith words, for what you say continually will come to pass eventually; your victory is embedded in what you say.

(28)

Better is not only contingent on what God is doing for you, but it is also based on what he is doing through you.

(29)

Some of your losses in the past will be transformed into gains in the future, just be tenacious and patient through the process.

(30)

Don't be afraid of having to start over again because this time you will start with some past experience.

(31)

Exponential growth is not always a derivative of how good a job you are doing, but sometimes it is predicated on how influential you are on those you are reaching.

(32)

When you are determined to stand out and be exceptional, the wise will admire you, the wishful will envy you, and the foolish will hate you.

(33)

Don't be afraid to take risks in your life journey, if you win then you can lead others and if you lose, then you can guide many.

(34)

Complacency is the enemy of achievements, just as fear is the enemy of faith. To get to where you want to go, you'll have to completely annihilate it.

(35)

When others say all manner of evil against you, don't retaliate because it's a common law that the tree that bears the sweetest fruits is the one that gets the most stones.

(36)

Take all that you can from life because when life starts taking from you, it will take even your last breath.

(37)

There is no tangible joy in victory without running the risk of defeat.

(38)

A path without obstacles will lead you to a place called nowhere, but a path with obstacles will lead you to somewhere.

(39)

It is better for you to focus on being effective and productive rather than just being busy and active.

(40)

It is our faith that encompasses our hope, it is our hope that diminishes our shame, and it is our love that eradicates our fear.

(41)

Faith is invisible, yet it is tangible and usable, and it will always work when we choose to work it.

(42)

Selfish and self-centered people don't compliment others because they oftentimes think that they are the only ones who deserve it.

(43)

Impoverished nations and their people don't really care how much you know until they know how much you really care.

(44)

Our knowledge will not impact our present posterity unless we impart it to them, so let's speak up, let's say something to them, let's share with them what we know.

(45)

Our God is great, and his greatness is unsearchable, so we have to trust him even though we can't trace him; he is altogether wonderful.

(46)

Our God is great, and his greatness is unsearchable; we all have to trust him even though we can't trace him; his ways are past finding out.

(47)

The difference between confidence and arrogance is that confidence says, I can do it with the help of the Lord, but arrogance says I can do it within myself.

(48)

You are not who others say you are, but you are what God has made you to be, so go on and fulfil his purpose for your life.

(49)

It's not everyone that starts out with you that will end up with you, be prepared for sudden changes.

(50)

Our existence in this life will be accompanied by many testings and trials, setbacks and difficulties; but we cannot avert these realities of life, so just go through it.

(51)

If your dream never scares you, then you did not dream big enough; the sky is not the limit, so think positively and dream big.

(52)

Don't let the negativity of others' opinions change the positivity of your final decision; go forward.

(53)

The positivity of your thinking will enhance the positivity of your saying, and the positivity of your saying will promote the positivity of your doing.

(54)

Never let the mishaps in your life determine the outcome of your life, learn to live laugh and love.

(55)

If you find yourself becoming hateful, then it's an indicator for you to get back to being loving, for when you share love it will be reciprocated back to you.

(56)

To the married men. If you connect yourself to polygamy and continue to reject monogamy, then you will end up in complete ignominy.

(57)

The people who are not endeavoring to go further are those who are satisfied with where they are.

(58)

Give a gift of absence to those who don't appreciate your presence and move on; they will surely miss you later.

(59)

Sometimes the people that you think are against you are not really against you, the reality is that they are just more focused on themselves.

(60)

As you go through this life, you will experience pattern changes, pendulum swings, trajectory rise, and Paradigm Shifts. Learn how to adapt to them and press on.

(61)

The real failures in life are not predicated on those who try and fail; but it is contingent on those who fail to try.

(62)

It is better to aim at a specific thing and hit than to aim at many things and miss.

(63)

Use the stumbling blocks that your enemies throw in your pathway as stepping stones to go a higher dimension.

(64)

Two natures lie within us, there is one that we should love and one that we should hate, but it is the one that we love the most that will dominate.

(65)

An optimist will envision a comeback while experiencing a setback, but a pessimist will always give in.

(66)

The positivity of your thinking will overcome the negativity of your hearing if you are relentless in your pursuit to achieve your goals.

(67)

There is no shortcut to genuine success; anything that you set out to do will take some doing, and everything that you set out to get will take some getting.

(68)

When you let pride and arrogance govern the outer you, then the soul will sink in the inner you.

(69)

Hating others is parallel to you holding yourself hostage in your own self-made prison.

(70)

Though we would differentiate in our opinions on many things, yet we still have to keep the camaraderie in everything; loving each other should not be an option, but it has to be a prevailing attitude.

(71)

If you try to be just like someone else, then you will become a cheap copy of a great original, so be who God has made you to be.

(72)

Leading without purpose and building without a plan will always be hazardous adventures.

(73)

Never let your passion transcend your gifting, work your gift and rest your passion; it is the working of your gift that will bring your blessings.

(74)

It is imperative that you learn to set goals and endeavor to achieve them, for life without goals is like a Merry-go-round with many activities but no achievements.

(75)

Don't let your past history affect your present victory or your future destiny; you are still a work in progress.

(76)

The things of your past are good for your learning, the victories of your present are good for your rejoicing, and the expectation of your future is good for your searching.

(77)

Learn how to use someone's no in their effort to block your progress as your Next opportunity in your pursuit for success.

(78)

It is good to listen to others, as they share their opinion, but it is your prerogative to adhere to your persuasion.

(79)

Learn to enlist while you exist, you are here for a cause, not just because, make something good happen for you, before something bad happen to you.

(80)

If you love to live, then you will live to love, for real living runs parallel with real loving, so love to live and live to love.

(81)

Give a chair to those who can't stand to see you blessed; maybe their jealousy will diminish when they are seated.

(82)

Your gifting may get you promoted, but it is your humility that will keep you grounded. Stay Humble.

(83)

No matter what others say about you or do to you, don't let anyone bring you so low as to hate them, learn how to hate the wrong in the person and love the person in the wrong.

(84)

In times of Prosperity and Prominence, your friends will know you, but in times of Poverty and Difficulty, you'll know your friends.

(85)

The best way to answer to your critics is with success, they will become your congratulators when you succeed.

(86)

If you can find your way without someone directing you then you have found the real purpose for your life.

(87)

Don't make a permanent decision over a temporary problem, whatsoever it is; remember that {This Too Shall Pass) just like the others did.

(88)

Self-confidence is oftentimes expressed in silence rather than in vociferousness; sometimes, your silence will reveal to others the things that you did not say.

(89)

Make the best of it in a bad situation, and cling to the fact that trouble don't last always.

(90)

Being joyful and ebullient is great, but it does not mean that you are free from problems and difficulties; it is just a good way to get over them.

(91)

In your times of great success, you will have many friends, but in times of terrible failures, you'll be like an orphan, love others for who they are and not for what they have.

(92)

Your present location is not your final destination; use what you have to get to where you want to go.

(93)

Every great achievement of today is derived from a thought of yesterday; it is a perspective that was transformed into an incentive, and then it came to fruition.

(94)

A great though without the necessary action is like a good seed that wasn't planted.

(95)

Impartation must be preceded by impaction, no one can distribute that which they haven't stored up; fill your vessel before you endeavor to pour into others.

(96)

To be successful in life, you have to plan your work and work your plan, for if you fail to plan, then you are planning to fail.

(97)

The best boss that you can have is you, so when you can't find a job, then employ yourself; the reality of it is that, you'll never get fired.

(98)

The people that are fearful of you going beyond them and doing better than they have done, are mainly those who will never support you.

(99)

You will never find that which you are looking for if you stop searching; you cannot be eligible if you are not available, and you cannot be called on if you are not present.

(100)

In most of your daily interactions, you don't always get what you deserve, but you will always get what you negotiate.

(101)

The order of redemption starts with the resounding question, "Where Art Thou?" If you can discover yourself, then you can become the person that you wanted to be.

(102)

Don't look down on others who are less fortunate than you are, unless you are going to lift them up, remember that life have a way of taking unprecedented turns.

(103)

Learn to enjoy the good times to the fullest when they are with you, because times and changes happen to everyone.

(104)

Tables have a way of turning. Situations have a way transforming. Patterns have a way of changing. Pendulum have a way of swinging. And Paradigm have a way of shifting. If you keep an eye believing, it can all happen in your favor.

(105)

Life transforming answers come with the ultimate questions (1) How bad do you want it? (2) Are You willing to make the sacrifice to get it? (3) Will you stay humble when you achieve it?

(106)

You don't need to change the system or the formula that is working for you, you just need to enhance it, because some changes can be detrimental, if it's not broken, don't try to fix it.

(107)

The saints of God are the privileged recipients of his wonderful salvation, but we can only become beneficiaries of his heavenly promises if we hold on to the end.

(108)

The biblical stipulations for our deliverance are unequivocal and indisputable; they are unambiguous and unmistakable, and we have to adhere to them and comply with them for us to obtain and maintain God's wonderful salvation.

(109)

We cannot authentically do the will of God, if we deviate from his divine plan and direction, where he leads us, we must follow, and where he send us, we have to go.

(110)

You have to pledge your allegiance primitively to God, in order for him to fulfill his purpose for your life.

(111)

Exponential growth in something that you are doing will not always derive from working harder; sometimes, it will come when you work smarter.

(112)

As exercise is beneficial to your well-being, and as darkness is conducive to sleep, so likewise is a positive attitude toward good health.

(113)

Every opportunity will have some difficulties, and every difficulty will have some opportunities, so whatever may tide you, stay positive.

(114)

When you learn how to become comfortable in your own skin, then your flaws and your weaknesses will not hinder you from achieving your goals and aspirations.

(115)

Your attitude is an inward feeling that is expressed by an outward behavior, it is an outward expression of an inward intention, it is your attitude that will determine your altitude, so make sure that you maintain the right one.

(116)

The difference between an obstacle and an opportunity is your attitude towards it.

(117)

There are many people who have great skills and much talent, plus wonderful ideas, but yet they can't get anything done because of skill, talent and ideas; without self-motivation, you'll still be afraid to take action.

(118)

Greatness will always connect to greatness, but misery loves the miserable company.

(119)

Being happy and content does not symbolize that you have all that you need, but it authenticates the fact that you are grateful for all that you have.

(120)

Greatness is predominantly derived from strong faith, courage, boldness, and audacity; you cannot become a great achiever if you are timid and fearful.

(121)

Disembarkation has always been preceded by embarkation; no one can get to their desired destination without starting on the journey.

(122)

The sustained growth in what you do will be determined by the continuity of your doing, so keep on doing what you have to do now, so you can do what you want to do later.

(123)

Real compliments are derived from heartfelt appreciation; learn to compliment those who you truly appreciate for what they have done in the past and what they are doing at present.

(124)

Don't let the negative sayings about you hinder the positive drive that is in you, but as they talk their talk, just keep on walking your walk.

(125)

Quit going to the places where you are tolerated and keep going to the places where you are appreciated.

(126)

Sometimes, when God doesn't allow you to fit in, it is an indicator that he wants you to stand out; exceptionality always comes with times of separation.

(127)

No one can genuinely uncovers their true potential until they have discovered themselves, and before you can be your true self, you have to first accept who you are.

(128)

Life changing answers will come with the ultimate questions; How bad do you want it? Are you willing to make the necessary sacrifices to get it? And will you stay humble and grounded when you have it?

(129)

Sometimes, all that you need to draw out of you what God has embedded inside of you is a motivational push from a family member, a friend, a brother or sister-in-Christ, or even a stranger.

(130)

The greatest source of encouragement that can come to you will come from you; so let your heart commune with your spirit, and learn how to encourage yourself.

(131)

He that finds a wife, has found a good thing, and she that gets a husband, has received a great thing; a good thing connected to a great thing is a marvelous thing.

(132)

The battle for our spiritual survival cannot be fought with carnal weapons, but it has to be fought with faith, hope and love. And for us to be consistent overcomers, we will need faith in our today, hope for our tomorrow, and love always.

(133)

Your past may be on the tongue of others, but your future is in the hands of God.

(134)

You will always struggle to reach your desired goals if you stop to answer to your critics along the way.

(135)

Don't become afraid of failing and having to start all over again, for this time you will be starting with some experience that you did not have before.

(136)

Mediocrity is unacceptable in the pursuit of excellence, learn to you what you do with the best of your ability.

(137)

Don't let your failures of the past suppress your victory of the present, nor your triumphs of the future, be positive and keep on pressing your way.

(138)

Impartation must be preceded by impaction, for no one can distribute that which they haven't stored up. Fill your vessels before you endeavor to pour into others.

(139)

Being joyful, exuberant, excited, and ebullient is great, but it does not mean that you are free from troubles; but it is a good way to get over them.

(140)

The mistakes and failures that cause you to become more humble are more beneficial to you than the achievements that cause you to become more arrogant.

(141)

In order for you to find yourself authentically, you have to come to yourself internally.

(142)

Your inner peace can be periodically disturbed, but it can't be permanently destroyed, so seek it more and more.

(143)

You cannot perpetuate evil in your effort to do good, for to do good continually, you have to be good internally.

(144)

No matter how tough life is, learn to give God thanks for allowing you to be alive, for where there is life, there is still hope.

(145)

When a flower is not blooming, you have to fix the environment in which it is growing, not the flower.

(146)

The fragrance of a flower spreads in the direction of the wind, but the goodness of God spreads in all directions, even against the wind.

(147)

No matter how bad your life situation is at present, you still have to be grateful to God each morning that you arise to see the dawn of a new day.

(148)

It is not every storm that comes upon the horizon of your existence that comes to disrupt or destroy your life; some storms come to clear your path.

(149)

You have to go through what you have to go through, to get to where you want to get to, there is no shortcut to tangible success.

(150)

You cannot be an overcomer of anything until you have been an undergoer of something.

(151)

No one can achieve their desired goals and aspirations unless they start the process; talk is always easy and cheap, but taking action will cost you something.

(152)

It is better to annihilate the cause of the pain than to alleviate the pain that is caused.

(153)

When we look into the totality of God's love for lost humanity, we have no other choice than to term it as incomparable and unparalleled.

(154)

As fathers to our sons, sometimes we spend so much time trying to feed them that we forget how to lead them.

(155)

Sometimes, the closer you get to your breakthrough, the more your warfare intensifies, but remember that the darkest hour of the night is just before dawn. So hold on; your victory is imminent.

(156)

Train your mind to listen to what God is saying in your spirit as opposed to what the Devil is shouting in your ears.

(157)

As human beings, we have to learn how to love people and use things, rather than loving things and using people.

(158)

God doesn't need our ability to do what He wants to do for us, but He needs our availability to do what he wants to do through us.

(159)

The ministry of the ministers should never be contingent on self-aggrandizement, but it should be predicated on the believer's edification.

(160)

When you come to a crossroads in your life, and you don't know which way to go or turn just look up and remember that Jesus is still the way maker.

(162)

You cannot be a person who make a great contribution in any area of life, and don't be criticized, criticism and controversy will be a part of the journey.

(163)

When the going gets tough, the tough got to keep going; giving up should not be an option.

(164)

A strong person will stand alone if he or she has to, but a weak person will always depend on the crowd.

(165)

The best thing about opinions is that everyone is entitled to them.

(166)

Don't strive to be powerful; strive to be faithful; don't just endeavor to be impactful, but also to be fruitful.

(167)

A ship is designed to take you places, so if your companionship, your partnership or your relationship is not taking you anywhere, then you have to abandon these ships.

(168)

You have to have some comparisons to know what you had before as opposed to what you have now.

(169)

It is only when you are completely healed from your past failures that you will be able to embrace your present triumphs and to look to your future victories.

(170)

You are better than they think you are, you are wiser that they thought you were, you are stronger than what they see you as, so strive continually to be the best version of yourself.

(171)

If you become totally satisfied with what you have, then you won't have any room left for the things that you really need.

(172)

Sometimes, the resounding yes that you were waiting to hear comes after the many Nos that you were tired of hearing.

(173)

One of the greatest lessons that you will ever learn is how to share love and receive love in return.

(174)

Love is parallel to the seeds that you sow in your garden; you will reap much more than you have sown initially.

(175)

Let the pain of your past be the power of your present and the tenacity of your future.

(176)

Your courage would be seen as great, according to the magnitude of the obstacles that you overcame.

(177)

It is the efficacious blood of Jesus that exonerates us and has given us the prerogative to obtain his wonderful salvation.

(178)

When we look at the totality of God's love for lost humanity,
we have no other choice than to term it as incomparable.

(179)

Fearlessness is an underrated quality that strengthens our
literal and spiritual apparatus to do more than we thought we
could have done.

(180)

Sometimes, our silence conveys more volume to our critics
than our vociferousness.

(181)

The failures of the past are not embedded in perpetuity, so
keep on believing in God for complete restoration.

(182)

No matter how high you go in life, there will be times of
turbulence, but when you think of the goodness of God, it will
remind you to be thankful.

(183)

When you try to be there for everyone that is connected to
you, you are running the risk of losing yourself.

(184)

When God is with you, the fiery darts that your enemies throw at you will always miss you.

(185)

The word of God is spiritual; it is educational and it is transformational; that's why we need to study it.

(186)

Whatsoever you depreciate in your life, it will surely decrease in its value.

(187)

The purpose is not static nor dysfunctional; it is dynamic and functional.

(188)

Sometimes, in your quest to articulate in a profound way, you lose the true sense of empowering others.

(189)

Maturity begins with the acceptance of responsibility, not only in the time of victory but also in the time of failure.

(190)

Identity crisis is derived from a personal crisis, if you cannot come to terms with who you are, then it will always be difficult to understand to whom you belong.

(191)

If the peripheries of your life take precedence over the pre-eminent things in your life, then you will not be able to serve the tangible purpose for your life.

(192)

Learn how to envision the false accusation against you as a free advertisement for you, and keep on moving.

(193)

Not everyone that is in your circle is truly on your team; some are self-appointed investigators who have a hidden agenda.

(194)

You don't need everything to enjoy your life; you already have a life to enjoy everything, so live, laugh and love.

(195)

Anyone can explain something to you, but no one can comprehend it for you; comprehension must be done in you.

(196)

You cannot authentically trust God and still be overwhelmed by fear and trepidation because fear is the enemy of faith and the destroyer of confidence, so let your faith conquer your fear.

(197)

Real contentment is hinged on being who God has made you
to be without anyone's permission.

(198)

Don't be afraid or lose hope in times of setbacks; it may be that
God is preparing you for a resounding comeback.

(199)

It is the same boiling water that softens the potatoes, that also
hardens the eggs; life is about what you make of it, not the
circumstances within it.

(200)

If you don't use your gifts and talents to initiate change, then
you may be seen as a part of the problems.

(201)

Many of the things that come easy won't last long, and many
of the things that last long won't come easy.

(202)

When you are totally engaged in a purpose-driven life, you
will be able to take less and do more with it.

(203)

Nothing is wrong with the environment of the people, but
something is wrong with the people of the environment.

(204)

Don't be afraid to ask questions about the things that you need to know, for what you don't know, can surely hurt you.

(205)

The dichotomy of our troubles in this life is something that we cannot avoid; darkness and light, good and evil, life and death, love and hate, but God has given us the prerogative to choose. It is our choices that will determine our destiny.

(206)

If you focus too much on your existing problems, it will hinder you from finding the best solutions.

(207)

When there are some very important choices for you to make, try your best to make the right ones so that you don't have to regret them later on.

(208)

Every day may not be a good day for you, but God is good every day, so trust him at all times.

(209)

Unforeseen circumstances can lead to major disasters, that's why it is imperative for us to plan our work, and then work our plan.

(210)

Your expected fruition demands immediate action to achieve it; you have to do the work in order to accomplish your goal.

(211)

Your total persuasion should always be the determining factor for your final decision.

(212)

A positive mindset will improve your habits and change the trajectory of your life.

(213)

Don't be a victim of your past; be a graduate of the lessons that you have learned from it.

(214)

In order for you to hear your inner (GPS) God's Positioning System, you have to turn off all the other distractions that are around you.

(215)

As you are dealing with the vicissitudes of this life, it is imperative to remember how far you came from to get to where you are at present. God is still able.

(216)

Unstable mindsets produce fluctuating personalities, but positive and stable thinking will help to restore your balance.

(217)

If you cannot be like a bridge to connect people together, then don't be like a wall to separate them; everybody needs somebody.

(218)

How can you say that you love God dearly and hate your brethren and your neighbours clearly?

(219)

Many of the difficulties that you are experiencing is not designed to hinder you, some of it design to get you re-focused.

(220)

Learn how to speak words of faith, for what you say continually will come to pass eventually. Speak it and claim it.

(221)

Competition is the enemy of completion; you cannot help to complete me if you are always competing against me.

(222)

In many areas of your life, it is your pain that will teach you that which your pride won't let you learn.

(223)

Your life span on earth is parallel to a fingerprint, which cannot be duplicated, so make the best of it while you are alive.

(224)

A strong person is humble enough to admit his or her mistakes, wise enough to learn from them, and tenacious enough to correct them.

(225)

You cannot change some of the things that you see around you, but you can surely change the way that you see things from within you.

(226)

Vision without action is just a hallucination and illusion.

(227)

In certain sports, your talent may win you games, but it is your teamwork that will win you championships.
Teamwork makes the dream work.

(228)

If you can't handle being talked about, then you are not ready for tangible success; criticism comes with greatness.

(229)

You are not a product of what you have been through; you are a solution to what you have survived.

(230)

Authentic partnerships are mainly built on differences and not just on commonalities; our relationship will be fine if I accept your uniqueness and you accept mine.

(231)

Gator-ade is good for vitality, and Lover-ade is good for your victory, so in your quest to get to your destiny, you have to use love without dissimulation.

(232)

The positivity of your thinking will enhance the positivity of your doing and improve the positivity of your living.

(233)

God has placed you in this world for a specific purpose; there is a God-ordained assignment attached to your life; make sure that you fulfil it.

(234)

Failure is derived from a feeling that evolved in you long before it became a reality to you, don't let the fear of it affect your faith to overcome it.

(235)

Delayed progress is a work in process, so don't abandon the project because of unexpected difficulties; stick to the original plan.

(236)

No one wants to be in a relationship without conversations and dialogue because the lack of communication is the road to separation.

(237)

Trust can take some years to build, but it can take a few seconds to break and decades to repair, so learn to maintain the trust that others have placed in you.

(238)

It is not what others have said to you or about you that will define you; it is what you say about yourself, so learn to speak to yourself with a positive mindset.

(239)

We all have had some bad times, we've had some difficult times, we've had some down times, we've had some tough times, but our God has always come to our rescue right on time; that's why we need to trust him, even though we can't trace him, for his ways are past finding out.

(240)

Learn to raise the trajectory of your confidence while you are severely tested because it will help you to endure it.

(241)

Reconciliation always works; it is the key ingredient that enhances tangible camaraderie.

(242)

When we endeavor to bring out the best in others, it will help us to bring out the best in ourselves.

(243)

If you can't resolve the problem, then leave it alone; don't be a prisoner to the things that you can't fix or change.

(244)

When God has chosen you, it does not really matter who rejects or neglects you; God''s favor will transcend all of your oppositions.

(245)
Learn how to trust your God-given intuition and instinctiveness in making your important decisions, remembering that your success or failure is contingent upon them.

(246)
Be willing to take action when you are persuaded about your plan; your continual action will eradicate every distraction.

(247)
Stop trying to fit in and be like someone else; endeavor to stand out and be exceptional.

(248)
You cannot flap with the chickens around you if you want to go to a higher dimension; you have to soar with the eagles.

(249)
Negativism is like an illicit drug; if you keep on sniffing it, you will become addicted to it.

(250)
Don't let others label you based on their assumptions of you, you are better than what they see you as. So keep your head up.

(251)

Being underestimated is a blessing in disguise because it always brings the best out of you.

(252)

Don't rush to be recognized; just work your gift to the best of your ability, and it will make room for you.

(253)

Creativity is derived from uncertainty, if you know your future then there is no need to look to it with great expectancy.

(254)

Success is predominantly coherent with success, but misery always runs parallel with misery.

(255)

There will always be a deficiency of genuine love in a marriage, when a couple make their decisions based on assumptions rather than total persuasions.

(256)

Evil cannot overcome evil; only good can do that, and hate cannot eliminate hate, only love can do that.

(257)

Many people would say, if God said it, I believe it, and that settles it, but the reality is if God said it, that settles it; whether we believe it or not, his word cannot be repealed.

(258)

Every day may not be a good day for you, but God is good every day to you, so thank him for his goodness every day.

(259)

Sometimes, we can be more affected by the silence of our friends than the words of our enemies.

(260)

Never try to decrease your goals, but always try to increase your effort in achieving them.

(261)

Preaching the gospel should never be predicated on personal aggrandization, but it should be always contingent on the glory of God.

(262)

When you are determined to stand out and be exceptional, the wise people will admire you, the wishful people will envy you, and the weak people will hate you.

(263)

The people that are lonely, are predominantly those who have a mindset to build walls of isolation, rather than bridges of connection.

(264)

You will always get more done when you make the days count than when you spend time counting the days.

(265)

Don't be afraid of pressure because it is pressure that transforms rough stones into beautiful diamonds.

(266)

When you are connected to direction, you will constantly reject distraction.

(267)

Stop trying to fit into everything that you are connected to; learn how to stand out and be exceptional.

(268)

Pain is not prejudice; it affects everyone that exists in this world.

(269)

Unforgiveness, animosity, and envy are parallel to someone who is drinking poison and expecting the person that they hate to die.

(270)

Don't doubt your ability, don't cancel your Creativity, don't limit your ingenuity, for these are the keys to your prosperity.

(271)

Learn to live each day in the present, and do all you can to make it wonderful because you will not always live to see another.

(272)

Be careful with your thoughts, for they can become your words; be careful with your words, for they can become your actions; be careful with your actions, for they can become your character; be careful with your character, for it can become your lifestyle.

(273)

To the unmarried woman, stop trying to find a husband, and start the process of finding yourself, for when you have authentically found yourself, then your God-sent husband will find you.

(274)

When you fall down, get up and brush off, straighten up, and keep on walking.

(275)

Don't let the difficulties of your present destroy your hope for the future; God is still in control.

(276)

You owe it to yourself to be consistent, you owe it to yourself to be disciplined, You owe it to yourself to be focused, You owe it to yourself to be faithful, And you owe it to yourself to be fruitful.

(277)

When you have crossroads in your life, and you don't know which way to turn, just look up and remember that God is still the way maker.

(278)

An act of great faith is taking the first step even when you cannot see the whole staircase.

(279)

Learn to appreciate where you are at present in your life's journey; even if it is not where you want to be, every season of your life serves a tangible purpose.

(280)

Your value does not decrease because of others' inability to see your worth, so hold your head up and keep your confidence.

(281)

Our everyday forecast always declares that the sun will shine, our God still reigns, and Jesus still save.

(282)

Whatsoever you feed it will grow, whether it is faith or doubt, courage or fear, positivity, or negativity; the choice is yours exclusively.

(283)

Stop competing and comparing yourself with others; God has placed you in the world to be your own unique self, so don't try to be a cheap copy of a great original.

(284)

Sometimes, the smallest step that you take in the right direction ends up becoming the most important step that you have taken in your whole lifetime, so tiptoe if you have to, but take a step.

(285)

When you start seeing the beauty of life, the ugliness of it will start disappearing. If you start looking into life with joy, sadness will start diminishing; if you go through your day-to-day life with a positive mindset, negativity will start subsiding.

(286)

Don't get vexed with someone for being who they always have been, but be upset with yourself for not coming to terms with it earlier.

(287)

Sometimes holding on to certain things can cause you more harm than if you let it go, if it is not good to you, then it won't be good for you.

(288)

When you are not healed from what hurt you, then you can find yourself bleeding on the people that didn't harm you.

(289)

If your gift runs parallel with your passion, it will be easier for your plan to come to fruition.

(290)

You will always do better in the things that you consistently challenge yourself to do.

(291)

Never place the keys to your happiness in someone else's pocket; always keep them in your possession.

(292)

Don't be afraid of failure, but rather be terrified of having to regret that you did not do what you should have done because of the fear of it.

(293)

Your career is what you are paid for, but your calling is what you were made to do. So look to the calling of God on your life and know assuredly that you were made by him to do what you are doing.

(294)

Nobody will have joy all the time, but everybody will have joy sometimes, so whatsoever you are going through at present, make the best of it.

(295)

Write your plan or your vision once it becomes clear to you, and you are totally persuaded by it, then the only action left is to work it. It will always work if you tenaciously work it.

(296)

Sometimes, you will be severely tested in a manner which may show your weakness, but when you learn how to endure it, eventually, it will reveal your strength.

(297)

Do what you do on a daily basis with a good Attitude and the right concept because, eventually, it will become your preparation for elevation.

(298)

If you get caught up in convenience, then you won't truly understand what a tangible sacrifice is.

(299)

Sometimes, people will invite you into their drama, and if you stay there too long, then their drama can become your trauma.

(300)

Don't waste your precious time flapping with the chickens around you, raise your trajectory and fly with the eagles that are above you.

(301)

If the l, me & my, of your life always take precedence in your life, then you will never be able to make a difference in other people's lives.

(302)

The real failures are not the people that tried and failed; it is the ones who fail to try.

(303)

In this life, you won't always get what you deserve, but you will always get what you have negotiated for.

(304)

Don't make a permanent decision over a temporary problem; your present situation will pass just like the others did; it's only a test.

(305)

You cannot become who you want to be without letting go of who you used to be, adjusting and adapting is the prerequisite of change.

(306)

You will only be able to prioritize your perspective when you truly know who you are and why you exist.

(307)

If you are committed to achieve your desired goals and aspirations, you will come to realize within the process, that rejection in one way, is direction in another way.

(308)

Don't let the negativity of others' opinions change the positivity of your final decision.

(309)

Authentic relationships are mainly built on differences and not just commonalities; our connection will be fine if your uniqueness is intertwined with mine.

(310)

If you continue to do what you love, and you really love what you do, with your complete trust in God, he will make way for you.

(311)

You cannot feel comfortable interacting in an environment that you have already outgrown; it is time for a transition.

(312)

Real victory is the derivative of a preceding battle that you have fought and have won.

(313)

Talk can always be termed as cheap, but taking action to back up what you say, will always cost you something.

(314)

A mediocre effort and preparation will not bring you exponential growth; for anything that you are doing, you have to give it your all.

(315)

God's extended mercies to us are not predicated on the good in us, but they are contingent on his love for us.

(316)

You cannot do things preposterously and expect great results or resounding victories.

(317)

Divisions and defamation are tools of destruction, but collaboration and congregation are tools of elevation.

(318)

If you want to go to a higher dimension, then you have to let go of every weight that is holding you back.

(319)

We can fight in a battle and win individually, but for us to win a war, we have to fight collectively.

(320)

The best policy for your spiritual longevity is your continual transparency; don't fake it to make it; be real.

(321)

Don't be pessimistic about your foreseeable future because your worst are behind you and your best days are before you.

(322)

Learn how to see the false accusation against you as a free advertisement for you, and keep on moving.

(323)

It is not everyone who is in your circle that is truly on your team; some are self-appointed investigators.

(324)

Anyone can explain something to you, but no one can comprehend it for you; the comprehension must be done in you.

(325)

When you are totally and wholeheartedly engaged in a purposed-riven life, you will take less and do more with it.

(326)

Sometimes, we have to realize that nothing is wrong with the environment of the people, but something is wrong with the people of the environment.

(327)

Don't be afraid to ask questions about the things that you need to know, for what you don't know can hurt you.

(328)

A positive mindset will improve your habits and change the trajectory of your life.

(329)

Don't be a victim of your past, but rather, be a graduate of the lessons that you have learned from it.

(330)

As you deal with the vicissitudes of life, it is imperative that you remember how far you came from to get to where you are at present. God is still able.

(331)

In order for you to hear your inner GPS, God's Positioning System, clearly, you have to turn off all the other devices that are distracting you.

(332)

If your confidence is derived from the applause of others, then your strength will always fluctuate; self-confidence is the pre-eminent thing that you need.

(333)

Learn how to speak the words of faith with confidence, for what you say continually will come to pass eventually.

(334)

The thing that you believe God for continue to see it by faith, continue to speak it by faith, and continue to claim it by faith.

(335)

Your positive attitude is the elevator to your desired altitude, the way that you think, will determine how high you go.

(336)

The paradigm shift that you need in your life must start in your mind, for where the mind goes, the body will follow.

(337)

Competition is the enemy of completion; you cannot help to complete me if you are always competing against me.

(338)

The pattern changes that you need in your life must start in your mind, for where the mind goes, the body will follow.

(339)

In many areas of your life, it is your pain that will help to teach you the things that your pride won't let you learn.

(340)

In sports, your talent may win you some games, but it is your teamwork that will win you championships.

(341)

If you can't handle being talked about, then you are not ready for tangible success; criticism comes with greatness.

(342)

You are not a product of what you have been through, you are a living witness of the things you have survived.

(343)

Real partnerships are mainly built on differences and not just on commonalities; our connection will be fine if your uniqueness is intertwined with mine.

(344)

Trust can take years to build, but it can take seconds to break, and decades to repair. Learn to maintain the trust that others have placed in you.

## (345)

It is not what others say about you that will define you; it is what you say about yourself that will, so learn to commune with your own heart from a positive mindset.

## (346)

Be willing to take action when you are persuaded about your plan; your continual action will defy every distraction.

## (347)

Let go of the things that are keeping you back and hold on to the things that are taking you forward.

## (348)

Stop trying to fit in and be average; endeavor to stand out and be exceptional.

## (349)

Just because the truth of God's infallible word is not as popular as it ought to be means that we should stop declaring it, no we can't stop because the word still works.

## (350)

Don't let the foolishness of you, destroy the disposition that is embedded in you learn to adhere to you God given Intuition.

(351)
You cannot waste your time flapping with chickens; if you want to go to a higher dimension, you have to soar with the eagles.

(352)
Success is predominantly coherent with success, but misery always runs parallel with misery.

(353)
There will always be a deficiency of genuine Jove in a marriage when a couple makes their decisions on assumptions instead of total persuasions.

(354)
Evil cannot overcome evil, only good can do that, hate cannot eliminate hate, only love can do that.

(355)
Many people would say, if God said it, I believe it, and that settles it, but the reality is, if God said it, that settles it; whether we believe it or not, his word is settled in Heaven, and it cannot be repealed.

(356)

We all had some bad times, we've had some difficult times, we've had some tough times, we've had some down times, but our God has always shown up on time; that's why we need to trust him even though we can't trace him.

(357)

You cannot authentically trust God, and still we are overwhelmed with fear and trepidation because fear is the enemy of faith and the destroyer of confidence, so let your faith conquer your fear.

(358)

If you want to go higher to another dimension, then a paradigm Shift is needed, a Pattern Change is necessary, a Pendulum Swing has to happen in your life.

(359)

The people that are lonely, are those who choose to build wall of isolation, instead of building bridges of connection.

(360)

You will always get more done when you make the days count, than when you spend time counting the days.

(361)

Don't be afraid of pressure because it is pressure that transforms rough stones into beautiful diamonds.

(362)

Live each day in the present and do all that you can to make it a wonderful day because you will not always live to see another.

(363)

If you wholeheartedly believe that your life is worthwhile living, then you will do your best to live it well.

(364)

An act of great faith is embedded in taking the first step, even though you cannot see the entire staircase.

(365)

Your value does not decrease because of someone's inability to see your worth, so hold your head up and keep your confidence.

(366)

Our everyday life forecast always declares that the sun will shine, our God still reigns, and Jesus still saves.

(367)

Your present difficulty may seem like it is insurmountable, but God is still able to resolve it; just keep on believing that in his own time, he will.

(368)
The authenticity of your thanksgiving is derived from your daily thanks living, people who live in thanks will always find it easy to give thanks.

(369)
It is the tough situations in your life that will help you to discover things about yourself that you did not know were embedded inside of you.

(370)
Whatsoever you feed, it will grow, whether it's Faith or Doubt, Courage or Fear, Positivity or Negativity; it is your choice.

(371)
Don't get vexed with someone for being who they always have been, but be upset with yourself for not coming to terms with it earlier.

(372)
Sometimes, holding on to certain things will cause you more harm than if you let them go; if they are not good to you, then they cannot be good for you.

(373)
When you are not totally healed from what has hurt you, you can find yourself bleeding on the people who did not harm you.

(374)

When you start to see the beauty of life, the way that it should be seen, then the ugliness of it will start disappearing.

(375)

If you go through your day with a positive mindset, negativity will start subsiding.

(376)

As a Christian, whenever the task before you is really hard, and it seems to be insurmountable, it means that it is orchestrated by God.

(377)

When your gift runs parallel with your passion, it will be much more easier for your plan to come to fruition.

(378)

Learn to write your vision and make it plain, for once it becomes clear to you, then you just have to work on it. It will work if you tenaciously work it.

(379)

Don't be too quick to gravitate to something that you have heard or read about until you have proven that it is facts and not fiction.

(380)

Literal conformity will bring forth spiritual travesty, so don't be conformed to the philosophies of this world but be transformed by the renewing of your mind through the word of God.

(381)

Your gifting and calling are always embedded in the things that you genuinely care about.

(382)

Don't be quick to gravitate to something that you have heard or read about until you have proved that it is facts and not fiction.

(383)

There is no shortcut to tangible success; you have to go through what you have to go through to get to the place that you want to get to.

(384)

The Epiphany of our salvation is a complete derivative of the theophany of our great God.

(385)

Just because the infallible word of God is not as popular as it should be in this generation does not mean that we should stop declaring it. The word of God still works.

(386)

If you try to be someone else, you will become a cheap copy of a great original, learn to be yourself, you are one of a kind, there is only one you.

(387)

Never criticize a situation that you haven't experienced because it might become your biggest test somewhere in the distant future.

(388)

Don't start your day with the broken pieces from yesterday; every day is a new start and a new beginning.

(389)

One day at a time is what we should be thankful for, because we can't bring back yesterday, nor can we bring in tomorrow.

(390)

To the woman who is dating a man with a desire to get married, don't let him see you as a woman that he can get, but let him see you as the woman he can have.

(391)

Love is more vastly received when it is genuinely and continually expressed, so if you need love, then share love.

(392)

Before you assume, get the facts; before you judge, get to know why; and before you speak, think things over.

(393)

No matter how many times you have failed before, God can make the rest of your life the best of your life; just trust him through the process.

(394)

In your quest to achieve your desired goals, you have to feed your faith and starve your fear.

(395)

A good woman is not contingent on hips, lips and fingertips, nor her looks, shape and size, but it is predicated on her ways, her concept and her heart.

(396)

Learn how to spread love everywhere you go, let no one that come in contact with you leave your presence without feeling better.

(397)

Having an attitude of gratitude is one of life's most positive affirmations.

(398)

Learn how to control your anger because it is just one letter away from danger.

(399)

If you are not prepared to be criticized, ostracized, downsized, and scrutinized, then you are not ready for real leadership.

(400)

The reason why I praise God like I do, is because I don't deserve anything that I have, but yet he gave them to me anyway.

(401)

To be inspired by others is something great, but to get to the place where you can inspire others, is much more greater.

(402)

Stop being accessible to the enemy of your soul, and start being available to the savior of your soul, who is Jesus Christ the Lord.

(403)

Sometimes it is after you have suffered your most devastating failure, that you then became able to embrace your greatest victory.

(404)

You cannot allow your past to hinder what God has for you in the present and what he will do for you in the future.

(405)

One of the most destructive weapons that the devil will use against you is yourself; don't become the weapon for your own destruction.

(406)

Practice who you want to be in private; then, it will become easy for you to perfect it in public.

(407)

God has given to us the wonderful gift called life, and what we do with it will be the determining factor of our existence.

(408)

You are much more than other people's opinion of you, so don't let those around you label you or set the limit to your success.

(409)

If you cannot control your own spirit then you like a city without walls or protection, don't let the pride of you transcend the temperance in you.

(410)

Division, polarization, and degradation are invisible weapons of destruction, but congregation, collaboration and unification are tools of elevation.

(411)

Genuine change is not cheap; it will cost you death to the old in order for you to experience birth to the new.

(412)

Many times, our friendships and relationships with others arrive at a precarious place because we fail to fix the problems before they escalate into emergencies.

(413)

The difference between an argument and a discussion is that an argument alleges charges and blame, but a discussion deals with the ongoing issues.

(414)

The fear of rejection can paralyze you, but the joy of acceptance will enhance your strength and build your confidence.

(415)

Don't surround yourself with images of success to hide your secret failures; transparency is always the best policy.

(416)

Stop looking for change around you, and start initiating it from within you, endeavor to be the change that you want to see.

(417)

Don't prioritize the people in your life who have never tried to add value to your life; give preeminence to those who want to see you excel.

(418)

There are some things that you can expose, and there are some things that you can't, but there will always be some very important things that you'll have to keep to yourself in reticence.

(419)

Two natures lie within you, the nature of good and the nature of evil, but it is the one that you give heed to the most that will dominate your life.

(420)

Whenever you are faced with an insurmountable task, it means that it is time to turn it over to God; he specializes in the things that are impossible to resolve.

(421)

You are fearfully and wonderfully made by the Mighty hands of God, so sometimes you have to look at yourself in the mirror and thank God for the great things he has done.

(422)

Sometimes your family members and your close friends don't really need more from you, but more of you, so learn to read the different signals.

(423)

No one can give you what they don't have; neither can a warehouse distribute that which they haven't stored up.

(424)

Learn to invest in your abilities and giftings that God have entrusted you with, because waiting on others to establish you is a big risk.

(425)

If you have been privileged to achieve any level of success, then pour your knowledge into as many people as you can because success is only quantifiable when it is imparted to others.

(426)

The greatest compliment that you can give to your mentors is to put into practice the things that they have taught you.

(427)

You will never take the initiative in anything if you just wait to react to other things; initiation is the catalyst to innovation.

(428)

God has the power to transform your life from a great mess into Greatness. Just stick to his plan and purpose for your life.

(429)

You cannot have genuine friendship if you always hide your true self, it is your transparency that will enhance your camaraderie.

(430)

Self-confidence is better expressed in silence than in vociferousness. Sometimes, your silence will reveal to others the things that you did not say.

(431)

Oftentimes, what people need to alleviate their pain is not a brilliant mind that speaks well but a caring heart that listens to others.

(432)

To be kind is far more better than to be right, because kindness is the epitome of authentic love.

(433)

Greatness is always connected to greatness, but misery will attract a miserable company.

(434)

Sometimes you may get some things serendipitously and in other times, things may happen in your favor inadvertently, but it is dangerous to let happen-stance govern your life.

(435)

The continued success of a great company is not contingent on the numerous clienteles that they have, but it is based on the good service that they give.

(436)

You cannot have too much knowledge in any way, but you can have too little knowledge in many ways.

(437)

Balance is the epitome of real maturity; a balanced mind will always enhance your tranquility.

(438)

No one can stop you if you refused to be stopped, no one can hinder if you refused to be hindered, and no one can bring you down, if you are determined to stay up.

(439)

Sometimes it will take A common enemy that we cannot see, to bring us into unity with the people that we can see.

(440)

Be careful with your thoughts, for they can become your words, be careful with your words, for they can become your actions, be careful with your actions for they can become your habits, be careful with your habits for they can become your lifestyle.

(441)

Instead of worrying about the things that you can't control, shift your energy to that which you can create.

(442)

Don't talk yourself out of your own success, but think more, plan more and do more.

(443)

Sometimes the unexpected troubles that you are experiencing is an indicator that God is positioning you for what he has already prepared for you.

(444)

Your extremity is God's way of showing himself strong in your life, so just trust him, obey him and believe him.

(445)

If you keep doing what you always have done, then you will continue to be who you always have been.

(446)

The things in your life that cause you to live in hate are the same things that you need to eliminate.

(447)

Never allow pride and self-will to take the place of humility and genuine rapport in your personal life.

(448)

Don't let competition take the place of cooperation, or hate to take the place of love, or histrionic personality take the place of tangible synergy; keep your heart with all diligence.

(449)

Don't be someone's spare-time, part-time, or some-time friend, if they can't be there for you at all times it isn't worth wasting your time.

(450)

Because of the perilous age that we are presently living in, there are many things that we won't be able to comprehend, but we still have to be grateful to God and give him all the glory, knowing that it could have been worse.

Made in the USA
Columbia, SC
10 August 2024

39718071R00048